Boundaries Washed Away

Nikki Hopewell
Illustrated by Fiona King

Rigby®

A Harcourt Achieve Imprint

www.Rigby.com
1-800-531-5015

Literacy by Design Leveled Readers: *Boundaries Washed Away*

ISBN-13: 978-1-4189-3785-0
ISBN-10:   1-4189-3785-1

Printed in China
3 4 5 6 7 8 985 14 13 12 11 10 09 08

Contents

Chapter 1

Unfriendly Visitors

Juliette grabbed the broom and stepped outside to sweep the sidewalk in front of her father's produce store. She was hoping that after she finished her work, she could ride her bike in the Texas sunshine. However, she noticed several clouds overhead, and the sky was turning gray. Just then Juliette saw two of her classmates—Fernando and Hassan—walking in the direction of her father's store.

Suddenly Juliette's father came outside with a worried look on his face. He spoke to Juliette rapidly in Creole about news he had heard on the radio. The city of Galveston had issued a flash flood watch, telling everyone that heavy rains were about to fall and flooding was possible. By this time, Fernando and Hassan had stopped walking and were now listening to Juliette and her father.

Fernando and Hassan stood across the street from the store, laughing and joking in amusement. Juliette suddenly knew that the boys were making fun of her father as he spoke to her in Creole. They didn't realize that Juliette's father also knew English very well and understood that the boys were making fun of him. When Fernando and Hassan finally stopped laughing, Juliette watched angrily as they continued down the road.

"Try not to let them bother you, Juliette," said Papa kindly. Then he asked her to finish sweeping the front of the store so she could go home and enjoy the rest of the day before the rain began to fall.

Juliette was almost finished sweeping when her father came outside again. "The radio reports have made an adjustment and changed the flash flood watch to a flash flood warning," he informed her, looking very concerned. "That means that flooding has already started in certain areas, and it may be heading here next. We'll have to close the store early so we can buy supplies and prepare for the storm."

The two worked quickly to get customers taken care of and out of the store. Then they spent an hour moving things that were near the floor up onto high shelves.

Chapter 2

Getting Ready for the Rain

Before they left the store, Papa switched off the power. Juliette flipped over the "Open" sign so that the "Closed" side showed through the front window, and they hurried to the grocery store. After waiting in line behind many other people who were preparing for the storm, Juliette and Papa bought the things they would need: bottled water, canned food, batteries, flashlights, and a first-aid kit.

As they slowly drove home, the sky grew completely black. The rain fell harder and harder, making it very difficult for Papa to see the road. Peering through her car window at the pouring rain, Juliette asked nervously, "Do you think the store will be flooded by tonight, Papa?"

"I sure hope not, Juliette. However, if we don't get home soon, our house might be."

11

When Juliette and Papa finally arrived home and stepped out of the car, the water was already up to their ankles. "Hurry up and get inside, Juliette!" Papa yelled, wiping rain from his eyes and picking up their box of supplies.

As they closed the front door against the pouring rain, Juliette asked, "Papa, what should we do first to protect our house?"

"First we have to fill the bathtub and sinks with water in case our water supply becomes polluted," Papa told her. Once they had done this, Papa said, "Now we should move as many things upstairs as we can." He glanced out the window and, turning back to Juliette, said, "We don't have much time."

Chapter 3

Flood!

As Juliette moved the last of the dining room chairs upstairs, she looked out the window. The water flowing down the street had risen to the tops of the tires of people's cars. Suddenly Juliette thought of her Uncle Henri–Papa's brother from Haiti–who had recently come to Texas to work with Papa at the produce store. "Papa, do you think Uncle Henri is OK?" she called downstairs. "He's all alone."

"That's good thinking, Juliette," Papa replied. "I'll call him to make sure he's all right."

Papa picked up the phone and dialed Uncle Henri's phone number, but no one answered. "Maybe the phone lines aren't working because of all the rain," suggested Juliette.

"Then we should go check on him to make sure he's all right," said Papa.

"We'll need to stay very close together out there," Papa continued. "Let's put on our rain gear and be on our way before the water gets any higher."

Papa and Juliette quickly got dressed in their rain gear: rain jackets, rubber boots, and rubber hats. When they stepped out into the street, the water had risen to reach Papa's knees and Juliette's hips. Juliette was carefully wading through the water ahead of Papa when a thick, low-hanging tree branch started to bend under the weight of the rain. Just as Juliette walked below the branch, it snapped and fell, separating her from Papa. Papa shoved the branch to move it, but it was stuck. Soon the current was pulling Juliette farther and farther away from him.

Chapter 4

Swept Away!

"**J**uliette!" Papa shouted as the water rushed quickly around his daughter. Rain poured down on them and the water level continued to rise. Papa knew he had to act fast.

"Grab on to something, Juliette!" Papa called. Papa was using all of his strength to push the fallen tree branch out of his way, but it refused to move. So Papa held his breath and ducked under the water, beneath the branch, and popped up on the other side. Juliette was now just a few feet away.

Papa reached out for Juliette's hand, but he missed it as the water swept between them. Papa tried again to grab Juliette, but caught the sleeve of her raincoat instead. Just as he thought Juliette was safe, her raincoat slipped out of his hand.

All of a sudden the back of Juliette's raincoat got caught on a fallen tree branch and the branch stopped her from drifting away. "Papa," she shouted, "I'm OK!"

Keeping Juliette's yellow raincoat in sight, Papa rushed toward her. As he came closer, Juliette reached out and clutched his arm. She pulled Papa toward her, and then he was able to grasp the branch and steady himself.

"Papa, are you all right?" gasped Juliette, relieved to see her father.

"Now that I know you're OK, I'm fine," said Papa, hugging Juliette to him. "Now grab the branch and hold on tight," he warned her, loosening her raincoat from the branch to free her.

"Papa, how will we ever be able to get to Uncle Henri in all this water?" asked Juliette, watching the water rise higher and higher around them.

"We'll just have to think hard, Juliette," Papa told her. But all Juliette could think about or see was water. Water gushed everywhere around them as branches, garbage cans, and even shoes and books floated by. Juliette forced herself to focus on the problem, and finally she saw a solution.

Chapter 5

Trying Out a New Plan

"**P**apa, look," said Juliette, pointing to an object at the end of the street. It was a canoe that was stuck between the trunk of a tree and a nearby house. "If we can get to that canoe, we can use it to get to Uncle Henri," suggested Juliette.

"Now that's good thinking, Juliette," Papa praised her. "We'll have to move very carefully and swim to the canoe."

Juliette went first so Papa would always be able to see her. He followed closely behind her, holding the back of her raincoat to keep her with him. When they reached the canoe, they turned it over together. Then Papa slowly climbed in, pulling Juliette in after.

"Papa, how will we steer the canoe?" Juliette asked, realizing there were no paddles.

"We'll have to use some long, thick tree branches," answered Papa. He pushed off from the tree and slowly moved the canoe alongside it until he saw some tree branches in the muddy water. Nearly tipping the canoe over, Papa reached out to the tree limbs and with great effort broke off two long, sturdy branches.

Handing one branch to Juliette, Papa gave a final push from the tree trunk with the other and let the canoe move rapidly with the current. "Paddle as fast as you can, Juliette!" Papa yelled.

Through the pouring rain, it was hard to see where they were going. Papa and Juliette struggled to control the canoe and guide it up the street toward Uncle Henri's house.

Chapter 6

One Stop Along the Way

Suddenly Juliette shouted, "Papa, look at what's happening to the canoe!" The heavy rain was filling the bottom of the canoe with water. Juliette and Papa began rapidly tossing handfuls of water over the sides of the canoe. As they battled against the storm and tried to keep the canoe from sinking, Juliette heard someone call for help in the distance.

Looking up, Juliette and Papa saw two boys standing on top of a car that was underwater, waving their arms. Juliette and Papa paddled toward the boys, and soon Juliette realized who they were: Fernando and Hassan, her classmates who had teased Papa earlier that day. Hassan explained that he and Fernando were on their way to Fernando's house when the current grew too strong and dangerous for them to keep walking. They had climbed on top of the car, hoping someone would pass by and help them before it was too late.

Papa and Juliette brought the boat as close to the car as they could. Papa held the branch out for Fernando to grab and Juliette helped pull him safely into the canoe. Then Papa carefully held the branch out again for Hassan. But as Hassan reached out for the branch, he lost his footing on the slippery car and fell into the water.

Before Hassan could be carried away by the current, Papa quickly reached his hand into the swirling water and felt Hassan grab his arm. "Help me pull him up!" called Papa. Fernando was shocked that Papa spoke English, and his eyes grew wide with amazement. Then Papa, Fernando, and Juliette pulled Hassan into the canoe.

"Are you OK?" Papa asked Hassan, who was so surprised that Papa spoke English that he couldn't answer.

Chapter 7

Another Rescue

As they paddled away, Juliette explained to Fernando and Hassan that she and Papa were on their way to check on her Uncle Henri. Soon they arrived at his house to find that the water had risen halfway up to his first floor windows. They guided the boat near a window and saw that Uncle Henri was moving furniture upstairs, looking nervously at the rising water.

Papa tapped on the window to get his brother's attention, but Uncle Henri was so busy that he didn't hear a thing. "I'd better go in and get him," said Papa.

"No, let us go in," suggested Hassan. "You stay here with the canoe." Before Papa could disagree, Fernando and Hassan lifted the window and stepped inside Uncle Henri's wet living room.

33

When Uncle Henri turned around and saw Fernando and Hassan–two strangers–climbing through the window, he thought they were robbers. Therefore, he yelled at them angrily in Creole to get out of his house. Fernando and Hassan tried to explain that they were there to help, but that only seemed to upset Uncle Henri even more. Startled, Fernando and Hassan began backing away toward the window.

Papa helped the boys climb safely out of the living room window and back into the canoe. "We were only trying to help—not make him mad," said Hassan, feeling guilty.

"He is learning English, but he wasn't sure why two boys would climb through his window and into his house during a storm. He thought you were there to steal from him," Papa explained.

"Juliette, you and the boys will have to keep the canoe steady while I go inside and get Uncle Henri," said Papa. Climbing through the window, Papa greeted his brother and explained in Creole that the heavy rain was not going to stop and he was in danger.

Uncle Henri understood then that he must leave his house to find safe, dry shelter until the storm ended. He and Papa rushed to the window to climb into the canoe. However, when Uncle Henri saw Fernando and Hassan, he hesitated. Once Papa explained that they had only been trying to help before, Uncle Henri carefully stepped into the canoe.

Chapter 8

Safe at Last!

"Papa, I see people going into our school for shelter. Let's climb the hill and go there to rest," suggested Juliette, exhausted after paddling for so long. She knew that her school served as a shelter where people could go to find a safe place during emergencies.

When they reached the bottom of the hill, Papa helped everyone out of the canoe. "We're sorry that we said mean things about your father earlier, Juliette," said Fernando to Juliette as they walked toward the school.

"Yeah, he helped save your uncle's life, so it's actually pretty cool that your father speaks . . . What is it?" asked Hassan.

"It's Creole," said Juliette proudly.

"Is the language hard to learn?" asked Fernando, looking thoughtfully at Papa.

"It's not hard to me, but it probably depends on what you're trying to say," answered Juliette.

"Suppose I want to say, 'Thank you' in Creole," said Hassan.

"Then you would say, *'Mèsi,'*" Juliette told him.

Repeating the unfamiliar word under their breath, Fernando and Hassan went over to where Papa was walking with Uncle Henri. *"Mèsi,* sir," Fernando and Hassan said to Papa together, smiling gratefully. *"Mèsi* very much!"